102 Tips

for

Online
Meetings

by Roger Courville

102 Tips for Online Meetings

© Copyright 2013 by Roger Courville

Published by

1080 Group

Quantity discounts, reseller, site licenses, and/or distribution rights are available for both hard copies and digital (ebook) versions.

Please contact 1080 Group, LLC at info@1080Group.com or 1-800-476-1080.

Get a free bullets-to-visuals PowerPoint tutorial and template with a subscription to Roger's newsletter here:
http://www.1080group.com/offers/bullets-to-visuals/

CONTENTS

A Note from Roger

To suggest that online meetings should replace in-person meetings would be irresponsible.

If we observe the history of media, however, we find that any new medium of communication inevitably finds unique advantages in that new medium.

In other words, online-versus-offline isn't the correct argument.

Online meetings aren't a second-rate alternative to in-person meetings. Both are important to a competitive 21st contemporary leadership, management, and communication strategy.

This book has no anecdotes, blooper stories, theory, or conjecture. It's just a collection of quick tips to accelerate your success.

And I trust that this is true: If even one idea improves your online meetings (multiplied times all the meeting participants and multiplied times all the meetings you'll ever be part of), it'll have paid for itself many times over.

To your successes,

Roger & the 1080 Group team

Ways to Improve Stakeholder Value Beyond Saving Travel Expenses

It may be a no-brainer, but it needs to be said. I don't advocate giving up face-to-face connections, but many leadership, management, and execution activities can be accomplished virtually.

1. Save travel time

Yes, time is money. But for many, time is the more precious commodity.

2. Increase attentiveness

Video creates a sense of presence, and web conferencing tools improve interaction.

3. Include a remote executive o subject matter expert

Increase the team's access to knowledge sharing, vision, and leadership.

Increase sensory richness beyond a phone call

Many people's learning and communicating preferences are visual and interactive.

Use VoIP to save audio conferencing bills

Most web conferencing vendors have a flat rate for web conferencing that includes VoIP. Most organizations have long distance and conference calling bills that they wish were lower.

Improve interpersonal connectedness

Video is obvious, but many conferencing solutions have attendee lists, show you who is speaking, and make it easer to interact and collaborate.

Unexpected
Ways to Use
Web Conferencing

Before you used a mobile phone, you probably got along without it just fine. Now could you? In time, you may find that web or video conferencing ends up serving you in unexpected ways, too.

7. Save travel across campus or town

Need to just knock something down in 15 minutes? Sometimes you double your expended time for a local appearance.

8. Collaborate at the same table

Conference room meetings often include passing around the cable to the room's projector, transcribing handwritten or whiteboard notes and/or taking phone pics of them. Use web conferencing to save all that even when you're in the same room.

9. Use a recurring meeting for your daily "stand up" meeting

Many teams have daily "stand up" meetings that only last five o ten minutes.

Ideas for Better Meeting Invitations

System generated invitations are convenient, but they usually only include generic stuff about the mechanics of the meeting (e.g., the phone number, login URL, etc.). If you stop there, you're often leaving money on the table.

10. Change the subject line of a system-generated meeting invite

People make an "open this/don't open this" decision from the subject line of an email. Make sure the subject line is more informative than the system-generated one.

11. Put the most important action item first

Someone who's busy may miss something added at the bottom of the email.

12. Include WIIFM in the invite

"What's in it for me?" is a common reminder that people are motivated, in part, by self-interest. Example: Instead of "New benefits plan," consider communicating, "Learn how to save money with the new benefits plan."

3. Add explicit instructions to the body of the email

If there is something that is wise to do (such as a use a system test link to ensure the participant can log in), edit the body of the system-generated invite to include the appropriate instructions. Example: "Action Required: This meeting will start and end on time. Please use this simple system test to ensure you are ready. <include the link>"

4. POWER TIP: Let people know in advance that they'll be on camera

 Remember that many people will think of the online meeting like a conference call…and give themselves permission to not brush their hair (or whatever they're inclined to do or not do).

15. Send a reminder email so invitees don't have to look for it

Many online meeting platforms do not have automated reminder emails (like webinar platforms do). Send one anyway.

16. Be mindful of time zone differences when you schedule the meeting

Remember that many people either do not regularly deal with other time zones and, of those who do, often they're used to their email or calendar program adjusting for those differences.

17. Include a link to a time zone converter

Nevermind how simple it'd be for someone to search for a time zone conversion website (like http://www.timeanddate.com/worldclock/converter.html), you will get the occasional email asking.

Ways to Get Other Presenters Ready

Comfort levels vary from person to person, and just because someone has participated in a quantity of online meetings doesn't mean that they really know how to use the technology well to be more productive.

18. Prep presenters in advance

Remember that often people will avoid something if they fear looking foolish. Consider using a brief session ahead of time to l them know what to expect and do.

19. Teach new users only what they need to know

Unless the meeting's objective is to train users on web conferencing, don't make the meeting a class on conferencing. Save the training for another time.

20. Teach as you go

Don't spend time at the beginning of the meeting teaching people the tools. Explain what to do as part of the meeting.

Tips to Improve Managing Meeting Technology and Processes

Technology is never the end; it's a means to an end. That said, it's useful to think about what we can do to make it work for us more effectively.

21. Schedule the meeting via Outlook (or equivalent) to save clicks

Many solutions have add-ins for calendars. Schedule the conference in your calendar to save doing it two different places.

22. Know what attendees are seeing

The easiest way to help others is to have confidence you know what they're looking at. Do a brief with a friend and be sure to practice taking an attendee's perspective.

23. Learn how to use your "instant meeting" functionality

Life isn't always scheduled on a calendar. Collaborating in on-the fly virtual meetings will help online meetings feel more like "the way we get things done."

24. Save time with recurring meetings

For regularly scheduled meetings such as a Monday morning staff meeting, set up a recurring meeting in your conferencing solution.

25. POWER TIP: Use the same meeting ID and audio conference number for recurring meetings

 Not only does this save you a lot of scheduling time, it won't take long for most regular attendees to memorize the meeting ID and/or phone number. The result: They'll find it easy, if not easier, to hop in on the meeting or join while they're on the road.

Tips for Meetings with Mixed Off and Online Participants

Meetings that blend in-person gatherings with online meeting participants are the hardest to manage: You have meeting participants who are having different psychosocial experiences (what they see, what and how they hear, how they interact, how they get documents).

26. Try online only: Ask participants to join from their own computers

It is easier for presenters to engage meeting participants when all are "co-equal." For example, taking a poll, seeing an indicator of who is speaking or paying attention, and/or the ability to coequally type something into chat is impossible unless everyone has access to the tools.

27. Use an extra computer to see the room

Ideally each participant has individual access, and each individual's camera points at them. Position one additional computer to view the whole room.

28. Point a camera at the whiteboard

Are you going to collaborate or take notes on a whiteboard? Set up your meeting so that virtual participants can see.

29. Appoint a group moderator

For the in-person audience, appoint one person to monitor and manage chat/Q&A.

30. Plan how to deal with documents

What is distributed to participants now will have to accommodate both on and offline participants.

31. Plan how you will collaborate

If someone draws on a whiteboard in the conference room, how will online participants see it?

Things to Do to Improve Satisfaction with Online Meetings

You will never hear me or my team argue that online meetings should entirely replace in-person meetings—that'd be irresponsible. Turning online meetings into an additional strategic asset in your organization, however, has a lot to do with whether or not you can help others find online meetings a satisfactory way to get work done.

32. Plan to start late

Starting a meeting late isn't a good custom, BUT… What doesn't feel like "late" in an in-person meeting does online. One solution: Tell everybody the meeting will commence at "5 minutes past."

33. Ask people to login early to ensure connectivity

Fortunately technical issues are infrequent, but it's not only frustrating for the participant having problems, it's frustrating for everyone else who is kept waiting.

34. Put up a welcome slide that tells people they're in the right place

Remember, just because someone connects their computer early doesn't mean they have to sit there and chitchat. This is n only reassuring for those who have less experience with online meetings, but you can give additional instructions such as, "We appreciate your courtesy in being ready for this meeting. Refill your coffee and get that last email done. We'll start promptly at 10:05am!"

5. Share a web-based countdown timer

Taking a break? Purposefully starting at a few minutes past the top of the hour to let participants get settled in? Try screen-sharing a countdown timer like http://www.online-stopwatch.com/countdown-timer (and be sure to start promptly thereafter!).

6. Teach attendees how to mute/unmute themselves

Background noise is especially distracting in online meetings. Empower participants with the knowledge and responsibility to be good online meeting citizens.

7. Let participants know how to be present and participatory

Some meeting participants will find adapting to online meetings to be second nature… and others won't. Guide their experience.

38. Let participants know you're recording

In some cases this is actually a legality, and I'm not the expert on this subject. But if you knew you were being recorded, it very well might change the tone you use when talking about someone or something, right? Give your participants the courtesy of letting them know.

Tips for Improving Mobile Meetings

The sale of web-enabled mobile devices now exceeds the number of PCs being sold. The question isn't *if* you will need to accommodate them for online meetings, it is *when*.

39. Determine the requirements for mobile participants

Some conferencing solutions may require mobile users (e.g., Android or iOS devices) to download a separate app from the app store. If so, you may benefit by letting participants know in advance.

40. Give additional attention to muting/unmuting

Mobile users are more likely to be in environments that have higher levels of background noise.

1. Design the "user experience" of your meeting with mobile in mind

Mobile participants may or may not have the same features (e.g., ability to type chat messages).

2. Design slides with mobile in mind

Many mobile users can "pinch" and "zoom" to change the size of their viewing area. Even so, presentation design choices such as font size are worth taking into account.

Ideas for Adapting In-Person Activities to Online Meetings

Changing the medium of communicating does one of three things: the offline activity translates perfectly, it doesn't translate at all, or it works with a little adaptation. Here are a few ideas of taking what we do offline and making it work online.

43. Use public chat as a tool for brainstorming ideas

Brainstorming often takes the form of everyone using sticky notes, or a note-taker capturing ideas on a whiteboard. Chat saves transcription, everyone can see clearly, and it's easier for one participant to comment on another participant's submission

44. Save public chat digitally to save re-typing notes

Some conferencing tools automatically save or give you the option to save meeting chat. Even if it doesn't, you can copy-paste. Either way, you save a lot of transcription (and handwriting interpretation!).

45. Use private chat like whispering to the person sitting next to you

Normal meeting behavior includes making comments to the person sitting next to you (that aren't intended for the whole room). It's even easier online, because now you can chat privately with anyone.

46. Pass screen sharing to a different presenter

In a conference room, having a second presenter involves either 1) coordinating in advance to get all presentations onto a single computer or 2) unplugging the projector from one person's computer and plugging in another person's computer. Online? "Change presenter" and you're done.

Ways to Improve Meeting Management

Much of meeting management is a function of people skills, and what we're NOT going to endeavor to do here is to tell you what to do about that one know-it-all who won't shut up (we've got those problems online or off!). When it relates to audio/web/video conferencing, here are a few ideas.

47. Turn features on and off

Just because a feature exists doesn't mean it should be on all the time. Professional conferencing solutions let you choose. For instance, maybe video is just used at the beginning of the meeting, or you turn on the hand-up feature for Q&A.

48. Log on early to "open" the meeting

With your conferencing solution, what happens if one of the meeting participants arrives early? Sometimes they get a message saying the meeting hasn't started, and sometimes they're put "on hold." If you start the meeting early, they'll be abl to chat (not unlike the small talk that occurs as people file into a conference room).

49. Open up chat so you can keep an eye on it (rather tha hunting for it)

Chat and/or Q&A panels are great for digital conversation, but feels less-than-natural if that conversation isn't real time. Keep chat panel open.

0. Use "mute all" to avoid background noise

Sometimes the presenter just needs to make a point for a few minutes (rather than have an open discussion). "Mute all" saves you the time and hassle of asking every participant to mute themselves.

1. Pause your screen

Need to go search for something on your hard drive? Pausing your screen not only improves privacy, it saves a lot of distraction.

2. Use chat to share a hot link

If you want to share a video or enlighten participants to a web-based resource, sharing a URL in chat is faster for participants. Many solutions make this link "hot" (clickable), and at worst participants can copy/paste into their browser. Either is easier than trying to type it into a browser while looking at your PowerPoint slide.

53. POWER TIP: Use an extra monitor or computer

 An extra monitor or computer gives you additional "real estate" for viewing participant videos, monitoring/ responding to chat or Q&A, etc. Different solutions work different ways, so it's worth a test.

3 Ways to Improve Attention

It's easy to think that we have shorter attention spans in online meetings, but many people are multitasking their way through in-person meetings, too. Nevertheless, there are things we can do to improve how we get and keep attention.

54. Keep the webcams on

Video provides a measure of accountability because participants realize you can see them.

55. Direct attention verbally by telling them what to focus on

Giving someone directions (a command) naturally triggers the brain. "Look at the upper right hand corner of this chart and you will see…"

56. Verbally instruct people how to use a tool or feature

In addition to the value of a command (in the previous tip), calling someone to action creates engagement. "We need to capture ideas for giveaways in the tradeshow booth. Use the chat pane that you'll find on the right-hand side of your attend panel to…"

57. Direct attention visually with a drawing or annotation tool

In the words of cognitive psychologist Daniel Willingham, "Change gets attention." We're wired to look at the thing that is moving.

58. Draw on a slide with PowerPoint's pen

Here's a tip conferencing companies may not tell you about. When PowerPoint is in full-screen mode, you can use Control-P (Command-P on a Mac) to turn your pointer into a pen, and Control/Command-U to turn it back into a pointer. Great when you're screen sharing.

59. POWER TIP: Differentiate participants with pointers and pens

 Conferencing solutions vary, but the better ones have ways you can identify the individual who is collaborating with you… changing the color of their "pen," a name indicator next to their pointer, etc.

60. Keep "presentation" or lecture segments shorter than in-person

In a shorter-attention span environment (the online meeting), e
on the side of interacting more frequently.

61. Ask people explicitly to avoid multitasking

Appeal to participants' sense of honor—ask them to focus on t
meeting. It usually helps to start on time, end on time, and avo
going off topic, of course…

62. Announce a break up front a a "release valve"

A break is like a "release valve." If you start the meeting and
explicitly note that you'll give them a break to get to pressing
email or calls, you'll have more luck with them paying attentio

53. Use speaking indicators to call on people by name

Web and video conferencing does something telephones don't do… give you an indication of who's speaking. Sometimes this is in the attendee list, and sometimes there are other indicators. Everybody loves to hear their name used, and you avoid guessing, "Was that Gina or Janine who just said that?"

54. Change your display name to how you want people to refer to you

Does your system log you in as "Stephen" when you actually go by "Steve" or "Skeeter?" Many systems will let you change this so other meeting participants can feel more comfortable, connected, or personable with you.

55. Ask participants to stand up and stretch

Crazy idea, right? We do it in face-to-face meetings, and it works in online meetings.

66. Use other tools, *any of them*, for engagement

Conferencing solutions have a plethora of variations of features. Hand-up indicators, thumbs up and thumbs down, checkmarks, emoticons, etc. Using variations of the ideas above, all of them are useful if you guide participants to adapt their offline behavior into the online environment.

Ways to Use an Agenda Better than a PowerPoint Slide

PowerPoint is often the de facto place we put an agenda. The trouble is that once we get past it, it's not editable or able to be referenced.

67. Use a Word (or equivalent) document as an "active" working agenda

Use screen sharing to show the Word document. Update it on-the-fly, and capture additional action items, or "parking lot" ideas that are outside the meeting's scope.

68. Use your working agenda as an ongoing record

Some types of meetings (e.g., a weekly team meeting) will reference things discussed in previous meetings. Pick up where you left off last week with the same document.

59. Combine the active agenda with other collaboration tools

Did you brainstorm or capture ideas in chat? Copy/paste those into your working agenda.

60. Send the document with "file/share" (or equivalent)

Word and other word processing documents let you email a file right from within the document. In Word this is File/Save & Send. However it works for you, it saves steps in sharing meeting notes and action items.

Ideas for Getting More Out of Your Camera

Video conferencing is a powerful part of feeling connected in a virtual meeting. Here are a few ideas for getting the most out it (and avoiding a few "oops" along the way).

71. Adjust gestures and expressions for the camera's eye

In a 1200-person study I conducted in 2011, the number one complaint about video conferencing leaders (by video conferencing attendees) was "distracting mannerisms or gesture

72. Balance the lighting

Poor lighting can wash out your forehead, make it look like you' got bags under your eyes, and otherwise contribute to a lousy experience. You don't need to look like you're in a television studio. You do need to look appropriate.

73. Don't get too close to the camera

Web cams are "near field" cameras. In other words, the depth c field is designed for you sitting at the computer, but this also means that small differences in distance make a big difference in how you look. Too close and your gestures and expressions become even more exaggerated.

4. Be aware of what's behind you

Study participants commented that they're often distracted by trying to read what's on your bookshelf or whiteboard, by someone walking by in the hall behind you, etc. Minimize distractions to improve focus.

5. POWER TIP: Make direct eye contact

 Think about how a newscaster "draws you in." They make eye contact with the camera. This is often unnatural in an online meeting since we're used to looking at our computer screen, not the camera—which means participants are looking at your forehead. "Eye contact" doesn't have to be 100%, but it's useful when you want to get attention and make a key point.

6. Show a physical object

Study participants actually noted this as one of their top benefits of video conferencing—showing something that's not otherwise on the computer screen.

Ways to Work more Effectively

Tools are useless unless you know the context in which they're used. What follows are a few ideas for getting "beyond the feature" to maximize productivity.

77. Assign the right privileges

You may or may not want every meeting participant to have access to every button or control. Managing access is key to keeping things flowing smoothly.

78. Work on a single document by sharing keyboard/mouse control

Common practice is to email documents back and forth, perha using "track changes" to manage changes. Screen sharing (alon is wonderful, but if collaborating on a document, it may be fast to turn over control of the document and let someone type ou their words.

79. Use a poll as a voting mechanism

It's perhaps obvious that you can vote using a poll, but two things are potentially better and easier online than off. One, yc can see exact percentages in the respondents (Offline, when y look out at a sea of hands, 42% and 38% look about the same) Two, many conferencing solutions capture poll results for pos session reporting.

30. Use a poll to take the pulse of the room

"Should we focus on X, Y, or Z this quarter?" If there are four people in the meeting, you just ask them verbally. If there are many more, that starts to be problematic... but it doesn't have to be.

31. Use a poll as a Likert scale

Even if you don't know the name or use, you've likely experienced a Likert scale (en.wikipedia.org/wiki/Likert_scale). It's one of those "on a scale of one to seven..." types of measurements. Instead of a poll being multiple choice, it could be a range from "strongly disagree" to "strongly agree."

32. Save a whiteboard with a screenshot for future reference

Not every conferencing solution has a whiteboard feature, and those who do may or may not let you save the work. No worries. You can draw/whiteboard on a blank PowerPoint slide (see that tip in 13 Ways to Improve Attention). Then just take a screenshot of it.

83. Consider the best place to share other documents

Some conferencing solutions have the ability to share documents, some don't. Nonetheless, handing out something during the meeting is going to leave out those who missed the meeting. You could save playing email tag by simply using cloud based storage instead (e.g., Dropbox, Sharefile, Sharepoint, etc.).

84. Keep participants "in the room" by sharing a live website

Some conferencing systems will let you take participants to a live URL. This is different than showing it to them with screen sharing... it actually takes them to an interactive web site inside the frame of conferencing controls. This is useful when you want to take them to a place to fill out a form (or whatever), but keep them from wandering off elsewhere on the web.

Tips for Hearing and Being Heard

For 100 years we've had the telephone as the way we had live, at-a-distance interactions. Even though we've added web and video conferencing to it, hearing and being heard still tends to be the backbone of virtual meetings.

85. Offer attendees a choice of both telephone and VoIP

VoIP (voice over internet protocol) is better than it has ever been but some participants may not be fully prepared to utilize it. A choice of both is fine.

86. Use USB headsets instead of computer microphone and speakers

Quality of the microphone and speakers in computers varies widely. USB headsets will help you sound better, hear better, and avoid feedback.

37. Use your mobile phone earbuds if no headset is available

Using your mobile phone earbuds helps you hear more effectively, and it prevents a feedback loop from occurring between the mic and speakers.

8. Skip the speaker phone

Speaker phones might be convenient (relative to the handset), but they are designed to pick up sound omnidirectionally (all directions). This introduces extra noise (every rattled paper, the air conditioning when it comes on, etc.). If someone is listening via their (lousy) computer speakers, it compounds the problem of poor sound.

Ideas for Troubleshooting

Most of the time online meetings are trouble-free. Something going wrong is never convenient, and often it's painful. There are so many variables that it's impossible to have a complete "if this, then do this" list. You have to think on your feet. Here's what I recommend.

89. Give yourself a little grace

Remember there are two categories of problems: Things you can do something about, and there are things that happen that you CAN'T do something about. In an offline analogy, if the light bulb in the conference room projector goes out, you learn to dance.

90. Start a "what if" notebook

If the electricity goes out, what are you going to do? Capture those ideas into your own "what to do if…" document. You won't have every answer nailed instantly, but it will guide you thinking through what steps you'll take.

91. Start with "who?"

If someone lets you know they're experiencing a difficulty, start with "who?" Is it just that person? Is it everybody? What action you decide to take will depend on the overall impact to your meeting. For instance, if "Joe" is all alone in not being able to log into the web conference but can still hear on the telephone, you might just move on instead of spending everybody's time helping Joe figure it out.

2. Ensure correct permissions

Some organizations block employees from downloading or installing any software. Web conferencing solutions work very differently. If unsure, ask invitees to use a link to test their computer in advance.

3. POWER TIP: Deal with audio feedback

 Audio feedback happens when there's a "closed loop" (the output of a speaker feeds into the microphone (an input). If it's bad, mute everyone. Then unmute them one-by-one. If it's tolerable, ask participants to mute/unmute themselves. If you can't isolate whose connection is causing the feedback, manage it by asking people to stay on mute except when speaking. If you can figure out who it is, ask them to use the telephone to dial in.

4. Make sure you have enough "chairs"

Conferencing solutions have an upper limit of how many people can be in the meeting at one time. Five minutes into the meeting is not when you want to discover this accidentally.

95. Beware what you show via screen sharing

Sharing your computer screen is an invitation for all participants to see your popups and notifications (e.g., Outlook, Twitter, Dropbox, et al). Spare yourself the embarrassment of having you friend instant message you with, "Hey dude, you SO shoulda kep your pants on last night."

96. POWER TIP: Use screen sharing for specific application or document

 Investigate whether or not your conferencing solution allow you to share only a specific application or document (instead of your entire desktop). The benefit that you may save an embarrassing mistake. The downside is that it will take longer to switch between different things you want to show and share.

97. Check graphics and fonts in advance

Some systems have you upload your PowerPoint or other document types into the room, and this sometimes can mess with graphics or fonts. Test it. You've been warned.

98. Test outside resources in advance

If pointing people to a video outside the conferencing solution (e.g., YouTube), let them know in advance. The last thing you want is to say, "Let's watch this video" only to discover that their firewall blocks YouTube.

Ideas for Improving Post-Meeting Management

Congratulations! You've just been part of transforming the world of work! Here are a few additional things to pay attention to.

99. Know the system requirements for the meeting recording

Conferencing systems often create recordings that have differen technical requirements.

100. Decide if you need to save the recording

Many conferencing plans do not host the recording file for you indefinitely. If it's important to preserve the recording, be aware

101. POWER TIP: Combine the follow up email with an invitation for the next meeting

 As you distribute the meeting notes, link to the recording, etc., include the attendance details for the next meeting.

102. Use a simple, anonymous survey to get feedback

Free solutions such as SurveyMonkey.com make it easy and, if you desire, anonymous for respondents to share ideas for how to improve. The key to improving response is to communicate clearly that it will only take a moment of their time.

Connect with Roger personally

LinkedIn: www.linkedin/in/rogerc

Facebook: www.facebook.com/valuesleuth

Twitter: www.twitter.com/rogercourville

Google Plus: plus.google.com/108906956266454929117/posts

Connect with 1080 Group on Twitter

1080 Group: www.twitter.com/1080group

Tips-only feed: www.twitter.com/virtualpreso

Other Products Available

The Virtual Presenter's Handbook

Virtual Body Language:

Using Your Voice for Impact in Online Meetings

Visit TheVirtualPresenter.com/products to purchase.

Hire Roger

The perfect speaker for your next meeting or conference…online or off

All programs customized to your team's needs.

info@1080Group.com or +1.503.476.1080

"Roger is an effective, dynamic speaker!"

—Pamela Lyons, MCSE, MCT
The Queen of QuickBooks
www.queenofquickbooks.com

20155317R00045

Made in the USA
San Bernardino, CA
30 March 2015